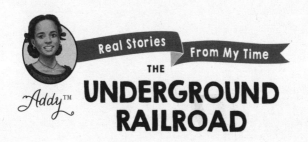

Real Stories From My Time

Addy™

THE
UNDERGROUND RAILROAD

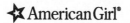
★ American Girl®

Real Stories **From My Time**

THE

Addy™ **UNDERGROUND RAILROAD**

By Bonnie Bader

With Addy Stories by Connie Porter

Illustrated by Kelley McMorris

Scholastic Inc.

Published by Scholastic Inc., *Publishers since 1920*. SCHOLASTIC and associated logos are trademarks and/or registered trademarks of Scholastic Inc. The publisher does not have any control over and does not assume any responsibility for author or third-party websites or their content.

Special thanks to Raphael Rogers

Photos ©: back cover: Library of Congress; 4: Map by Michael Siegel © Schomburg Center for Research in Black Culture, The New York Public Library; 13, 15, 22, 24, 26, 35, 36, 45, 47, 48: Library of Congress; 50: Schomburg Center, NYPL/Art Resource, NY; 58: The New York Public Library/Art Resource, NY; 63: Library of Congress; 71: Stan Rohrer/Alamy Images; 73: Schomburg Center, NYPL/Art Resource, NY; 80: Library of Congress; 92–93: Bettmann/Getty Images.

Book design by Jessica Meltzer, Suzanne LaGasa, and Charice Silverman
Photo research by Amla Sanghvi

Library of Congress Cataloging-in-Publication Number: 2017048126

 americangirl.com/service

ISBN 978-1-338-14892-3

10 9 8 7 6 5 4 3 2 1   18 19 20 21 22

Printed in the U.S.A.   23

First printing 2018

Real Stories From My Time

America's past is filled with all kinds of stories. Stories of courage, adventure, tragedy, and hope. The Real Stories From My Time series pairs American Girl's beloved historical characters with true stories of pivotal events in American history. As you travel back in time to discover America's past, these characters go with you to share their own incredible tales.

CONTENTS

Chapter 1

Not Really a Railroad

Thousands of slaves took the risk of escaping on the Underground Railroad. Each one of them has a story.

In 1830, a slave named Josiah Henson decided to follow the North Star from Maryland to Canada, where he could live as a free man. But Josiah could not flee alone. He had a wife and four children. Josiah's wife was overcome with terror at the idea of escaping. She was afraid that they would be hunted

1

down by dogs, brought back to their master, and whipped to death. Josiah insisted, but his wife resisted. She cried; Josiah argued. At last, his wife agreed.

On a moonless night in September, Josiah strapped his two youngest children in a knapsack and the family quietly boarded a small boat to cross a river. When they reached the shore, Josiah prayed that their journey would be safe.

For weeks, the family walked miles and miles at night. Whenever they heard a sound—a wagon's wheels, a dog **baying** at the moon—they hid. Soon, their food was all eaten. The children cried with hunger. Josiah bravely knocked on doors and asked for food. But the answer was always the same: No. Still, the family pressed on.

Josiah and his family hiked through the forest over fallen logs and branches, up and down steep **ravines**, and across fast-moving streams. At times they heard wolves howling nearby, but they remained brave. Once, a kind person gave the family a ride in a wagon. Another gave them passage on a boat.

At last, Josiah's family reached Canada. Josiah threw himself on the ground and kissed the sand. "I'm free!" he shouted. But this wouldn't be Josiah's last dangerous journey. Over his lifetime, Josiah helped approximately two hundred slaves find their way to freedom on the Underground Railroad.

The Underground Railroad did not run under the ground. It wasn't even a real railroad, with train cars and tracks, although there were passengers. The Underground Railroad was a series of routes and hiding places that slaves took to reach freedom.

No one really knows where the name

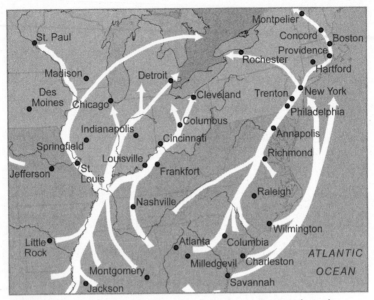

The white lines and arrows on this map show the routes people took to escape from slavery in the South to freedom in the North

"Underground Railroad" came from. One story was about a slave named Tice Davids, who escaped from Kentucky and swam across the Ohio River to freedom in Ohio. When Davids's owner discovered he was gone, he said that his slave "must have gone off on an underground railroad." Another story says that slave hunters in Pennsylvania came up with the name. And yet another story tells

4

about a slave who claimed he was making his way north, where "the railroad ran underground all the way to Boston."

Slaves desperately sought freedom and they would try to escape their harsh lives any way they could. Some walked hundreds and hundreds of miles. Others traveled by boat. Some were smuggled in a train or wagon. Most traveled at night so as not to be seen and caught.

The road to freedom was dangerous. If slaves were caught, they would be sent back to their master and punished. The punishments were horrible. But to many slaves it was worth the risk, for at the end of the road was a light—a light called freedom.

The fictional story of Addy Walker started in 1864, when Addy was nine years old. Addy; her older brother, Sam; her baby sister, Esther; and her parents were enslaved on a **plantation** in North Carolina. The Walkers lived in a tiny windowless cabin. They had hard lives in slavery. But they were together, and their love for each other gave them strength. Then the worst happened—Addy's family was torn apart, as enslaved families often were, when Sam and Poppa were sold to a different owner. Addy's family was divided, just as the nation was divided, North against South, by the Civil War.

Although Addy is a fictional character, her story will help you imagine what it was like to escape slavery on the Underground Railroad.

Addy's Story

"The night is real hot and I'm sweating. On my pallet, I try hard not to move—I don't want to bother my brother, Sam, who's sleeping at my feet, or baby Esther at my side. Flies buzz in my ears. I can hear more buzzing—a different kind. Momma and Poppa whispering. I want to hear what they're sayin', but I know I best keep still and pretend I'm asleep.

"Poppa get up and walk 'cross the dirt floor. He tell Momma we need to run away from Master Stevens's plantation. Poppa say the time is right to take our freedom. He wants us to run to the North. But Momma don't want to go.

"Then Poppa say Uncle Solomon tell him of railroad tracks near ten miles up the road. Uncle Solomon say we should follow them north till they cross another set of tracks. Where they cross, look for a house with red shutters. That's a **safe house**. An old white woman live there, name Miss Caroline, and she gonna help us.

"I'm scared as I listen to Poppa talk. Almost too scared to breathe. Was we really going to run away and take a train north to freedom? I never seen a train, but I want to. I'm scared, but I'm ready for my family to live free."

Chapter 2

Slavery in America

How did slavery start in America? In 1619, twenty Africans were brought to Jamestown, Virginia. The Africans were kidnapped from their homes. They did not want to come to Virginia at all. At home they were free. In Virginia they would be forced to work. They would not be paid. They would be beaten and sometimes starved. They would have no rights at all. Africans continued to arrive at the **colonies**, and by 1641 they were referred to as slaves.

When slaves were stolen from their homes in Africa, they were forced aboard ships. The journey across the Atlantic Ocean was called the **Middle Passage**. The trip could take anywhere from four to twelve weeks. Sometimes the slaves were "loosely packed" on the ships, which gave them more space and air to breathe. Ship captains thought that with more space and air, the slaves would be healthier when they got to North America. And a healthier slave meant more money. Other times, the slaves were packed in tightly—so tightly that they could barely move or breathe. But the ship captains didn't care. More slaves meant more money.

The slaves had chains around their ankles and wrists. When they wanted to go to the bathroom, they had to use buckets. The ships were filthy. Lots of slaves caught diseases such as smallpox. And there was hardly any food to eat. Some slaves tried to jump overboard.

Others simply stopped eating. For some, slavery was a fate worse than death.

Those who survived the harsh journey were brought to **auctions**, where they were sold. Here, white people examined the slaves and decided how much money to pay for them. The slaves were prodded and poked and pinched. They were treated like animals, not human beings.

African slaves on the Middle Passage journey

Once they were sold into slavery, they were forced to work without pay. Most slaves in the South worked on plantations. Some large plantations had as many as four hundred slaves. They planted, **tilled**, and picked the valuable crops—cotton, tobacco, and sugarcane. They worked under the hot sun, often with little food or water. Work began before sunrise and ended after sunset. **Overseers**, with whips in their hands, watched groups of slaves as they worked. Often, a slave was whipped or beaten if the overseer thought the slave wasn't working hard enough. Men and women were forced to work the fields—even pregnant women. And soon after their babies were born, mothers strapped their infants to their backs and got back to work. Even children were put to work.

Field slaves lived in small cabins with dirt floors. They were given rough blankets and maybe some straw to sleep on. Sometimes

Slaves picking cotton on a plantation in the South

families of ten people or more shared one cabin. Slave children did not go to school. Most never learned to read or write—it was against the law in most Southern states! Slaves caught trying to educate themselves, or their children, could be whipped or beaten—even the children.

Many slave owners lived in big fancy houses. House slaves had slightly better lives than those who worked in the fields. They cleaned, cooked, served food, and took care of their master's children. They also sewed and gardened. House slaves didn't live with their own families. They stayed inside their master's homes, where they were given a small room or maybe a closet to sleep in. Some house slaves learned to read and write. Still, house slaves were treated poorly and forced to work for no pay, and their lives were completely controlled by their owner.

Slaves often feared that their families would be torn apart. A plantation master could decide to sell a slave for any reason. Strong slaves could fetch a good price, as could an excellent cook or housekeeper. At any time, family members could be sold to far-off plantations. About one out of every five slaves bought and sold was a child under the age of ten. Children were often sold away without their parents. Once separated, most slaves never saw their loved ones again.

Slaves didn't only live on plantations. They also lived in cities and towns and worked in shops and businesses. At one time, slaves were in every part of America. In fact, twelve United States presidents owned slaves while they were in office or at some time during their lives.

By 1804, slavery was outlawed in Connecticut, Massachusetts, New Hampshire, New Jersey, New York, Pennsylvania, Rhode Island, and Vermont. In 1808, it became illegal to bring slaves into the United States from different countries such as those in Africa. But slavery itself was still legal in the United States. Slaves were still forced to work without pay. Their children were born into slavery, and the number of slaves grew. Generation after generation, they lived and died without rights. The only hope for a better life was to escape.

Plantation Life

"On Master Stevens's plantation, us slaves get up at dawn. We start working before the sun even up. I go out to the field with the other children to worm the tobacco. We got to peel off the big green worms crawling on the leaves so they can't eat the plants. Today, I ain't paying no mind to worming. The overseer comes over, whip in hand. He coming right at me, the buckles on his dusty boots clank-clank-clanking. I start to squeeze my eyes shut because I don't want to see that whip pulled back, see its angry hot tail about to rip into me. But as he come near, he drop that whip. He grab my wrists with one hand. His other hand got the worms I missed. Big fat ones, still live and wriggling. He stuff them worms right in my mouth. He tell me to eat them, chew them up. I chomp down on them. They burst in my mouth. They bitter and I gag. He stand there and make me swallow them. My heart is full of fear, but I don't show it. I don't even cry. When he ride off, I go right back to work."

Chapter 3

Abolitionists

The slave population in America grew and grew. By the time the Civil War broke out in 1861, there were around four million slaves. At this time, there were nineteen free states, where slavery wasn't allowed, and fifteen slave states, where slavery was legal. The slave states were in the South, where people had large plantations and needed lots of labor to work their crops.

The issue of slavery had divided Americans since the days of the **Founding Fathers**.

21

William Lloyd Garrison

There were heated arguments among government officials and among regular citizens about what to do regarding slavery. Those who opposed slavery and wanted to end it were called **abolitionists**.

William Lloyd Garrison, a white man, was one of the strongest leaders of the abolitionist movement. Growing up poor in Massachusetts, Garrison worked hard all his life—first as a printer, then as a writer and publisher. In 1831, he began publishing a newspaper called *The Liberator* that boldly called for the end of slavery. Many people did not like what they read. Garrison received death threats. The state of Georgia offered a $5,000 reward for his arrest. But this did not stop Garrison. He continued to speak out against slavery and became a cofounder of the American Anti-Slavery Society in 1833. Within five years, the organization had 1,350 chapters in different towns and cities throughout the North.

In 1841, a twenty-three-year-old escaped slave got up to speak at an Anti-Slavery Society meeting in Nantucket, Massachusetts. Trembling, he stood at the podium. Pushing his nerves aside, he delivered a heart-wrenching speech about the horrors of slavery. Who was this young man? He was Frederick Douglass, who would go on to write and speak out against slavery for the rest of his life and become an influential abolition-ist. Douglass spoke so well that some didn't believe that he was ever a slave. Most slaves couldn't read or write. So how could Douglass possibly do both? In 1845, Douglass pub-lished his autobiography, *Narrative of the Life of Frederick Douglass: An American Slave,*

Frederick Douglass

where he described his brutal life as a slave, and his struggle to learn to read. Publishing this book was dangerous—he admitted to being a slave, which meant he could be captured and returned to slavery. Although he was forced to flee to England at one point to avoid capture, Douglass continued his fight to end slavery. Many other free blacks—black people who were free citizens and not enslaved—also worked to end slavery.

Members of the **Quaker** church were also strong abolitionists. Quakers are a Christian group who believe that people should shake and tremble at the word of the Lord. That is how they got the name "Quakers." They believe in equality and were against slavery.

Many women were also active in the abolitionist movement. Sojourner Truth was one of the greatest abolitionists. Born into slavery in 1797, Sojourner was given the name Isabella Baumfree. She was not a slave in the South—she was a slave in the state of New York. Isabella was sold many times in her life. Her last master, John Dumont, promised her freedom, but he lied. So, at age twenty-nine, she took her baby daughter and escaped from slavery. While she was on the run, Isabella prayed for help. Her prayers were answered when Isaac and Maria Van Wagenen opened their doors. But John Dumont eventually caught up with her and demanded she hand over her baby. Isaac Van Wagenen paid John Dumont twenty dollars for Isabella and her baby, and Dumont returned to his plantation alone. Later, Isabella had a life-changing religious experience. She changed her name to Sojourner Truth and traveled up and down

Sojourner Truth

the land telling people the truth—the truth about the evils of slavery.

Besides preaching against slavery, many abolitionists also helped slaves escape on the Underground Railroad. They would hide slaves in their homes, in stores, and in barns. Helping slaves escape was risky—anyone caught hiding an escaped slave could be fined, put in jail, or even beaten. But many people took that risk. Abolitionists refused to give up their belief that all people should be free.

Ripped Apart!

"Right before we make our escape to freedom, the worst thing in the world happen. Poppa and Sam is sold. Master Stevens put Sam in a wagon, in chains and shackles. He tie a rag tight round his mouth. Poppa's on the ground, chained. I fly to him without wings. If I was an eagle, I would carry him and Sam away. I would fly all of us to freedom. But I am a slave just like them. I cling to Poppa. He tell me everything gonna be alright, but how can that be true? I hold on tighter—even when I hear the whip crack. It sound like a gun and hit me in the back like a lash of fire. I still hold on to Poppa, and Master Stevens say he gonna whip me again. Poppa tells me to let him go, but I can't. I will not let go! I will never let go! Master Stevens pull me back from Poppa and I fall into Momma arms. We both crying, crying so loud that crows fly up from the fields. Poppa not crying. He's put into the wagon with Sam. They loaded in like animals. The wagon pull away, and I worry I ain't never gonna see Poppa or Sam again.

"Later, I tell Momma I hate white people, but she tell me if I fill my heart with hate, there ain't gonna be room for love. She tell me that my Poppa and brother need me to fill my heart with love for them, not hate for white people. Poppa and Sam need me—I feel it in my heart."

The Passengers

Slaves often used code words to talk about their escape. A "station" was the code for a safe house for hiding. A safe house was owned by a "station master." A "conductor" was someone who led the slaves from station to station. And the runaway slaves were the "passengers."

Slaves found out about the Underground Railroad in different ways. Sometimes a runaway slave returned to the plantation in secret to help more slaves escape. Sometimes slaves learned about the Underground Railroad from other slaves. A **blacksmith** on a plantation might pound out a code with a hammer to tell the slaves when it was safe to take a chance on escape. And there were some white people who told slaves about safe houses.

Slaves decided to run away for different reasons. Often it was because they couldn't stand their harsh lives on the plantations. Slaves also decided to run away when they knew they were about to be sold and their family members would be separated.

When a slave made the decision to run away, he often waited until dark. If he could find a bit of food to take along, he would, but otherwise he would just leave with the clothes on his back. In the early days of the Underground Railroad, most passengers were men. It was especially risky for women and children to flee. Women and girls who escaped sometimes disguised themselves as men and boys.

Slaves had secret ways of letting their friends know that they were about to escape. Sometimes they passed their secrets by singing when they were working in the field. Their overseers did not listen to the words of the songs the slaves sang. "Let My People Go" was one song slaves often used to let the other slaves know that an escape plan was in the works.

The runaways often traveled about fifteen miles per night. They had no compass or map to guide them. When the sky was clear, they used the North Star to guide them in the right direction. When the sky was covered with clouds, slaves felt for moss on the forest trees. They knew that moss mainly grows on the north side of trees.

Since the Underground Railroad was a

secret, there were no written records at the time about how it operated, or what paths the escaped slaves took. But through word of mouth, slaves found out which way to go. Some slaves ran away to Florida. Up until 1845, Florida was not a part of the United States. In Florida, some slaves lived with the Seminole Indians. Other runaways joined secret communities hidden in deep woods or swamps. Some even ran all the way to Mexico. But most runaway slaves headed north to the free states or to Canada. They crossed swamps, rivers, forests, fields, and mountains. They were often hungry and tired and filthy, and they were always in great danger—but they pressed on to freedom.

Running through the countryside wasn't the only way a slave could escape. Henry Brown, a slave from Virginia, hatched a very crafty escape plan. Brown asked a free black man to construct a box for him. The box wasn't very big—only 3 feet long, 2 feet wide, and about 2.5 feet deep. The man drilled one airhole into the box, and Brown climbed inside with a bit of food and water. Nailed shut, the box was taken by white abolitionist Samuel Alexander Smith to a shipping company. Inside the box, Brown traveled by train, steamboat, ferry, and wagon. He

Escaping from slavery in Maryland

traveled upside down and sideways as the box was tossed about. He was scared and his head hurt. But when the box was delivered twenty-seven hours later to the Anti-Slavery Society in Philadelphia, Pennsylvania, and opened, Brown did not complain. He looked at his rescuers and said, "How do you do, Gentlemen?" From then on, he was known as Henry "Box" Brown. Although Brown's story

Frederick Douglass and other abolitionists watching Henry Brown come out of his shipping crate

had a good ending, Samuel Alexander Smith was later thrown in jail for helping Brown, and other slaves, escape.

Another slave who made a daring escape was sixteen-year-old Caroline Quarlls. Caroline, a slave in St. Louis, Missouri, decided to run away after her **mistress** got angry with her and cut off her long, dark, beautiful hair. Caroline had light skin, so she decided to take her chances that people would believe she was white. She did not run away under the cover of darkness. Instead, she boarded a ship headed to Illinois, saying that she was going to go to a school for young ladies. No one suspected that she was a runaway slave. Of course, once off the boat, Caroline didn't go to the school—she headed north, to freedom. But Caroline was in danger: Her master had spread the word that she had escaped. So Caroline had to find safe places to hide. She hid in people's homes. She hid in farms. She even hid in a wooden barrel. There was a reward for her capture, but with the help of conductors and safe houses, Caroline was able to travel through Illinois, Wisconsin, Indiana, and Michigan to reach Canada, where she was finally free.

Many slaves, however, did not make it to freedom when they tried to escape. Some became sick along the way and could not continue on; others simply gave up, or worse, were caught. Once the slave owner discovered his slave was missing, he would look for the runaway. He would hang up wanted posters all over town and take out ads in newspapers, offering a reward to entice others to help with the search. If the slave was captured, he or she would be harshly punished. Returned slaves were often whipped, beaten, or branded with red-hot irons. Some were made to wear iron collars with bells around their necks so their owners would know if they tried to run away again. Still, many did try to run away again, and again, and again, determined to reach freedom.

Escape!

"The night Momma and me make our escape, a full moon shine through the tall pines. We run from shadow to shadow, deeper and deeper into the woods. Sounds grow stranger. Owls screech. Bats swoop over our heads. Momma take my hand and hurries us along. I stumble over branches and rocks, roots and bushes. There's a dark shape in the bushes up ahead—when it moves, I scream. Momma stops and press her hand over my mouth. My screams put us in danger. Esther couldn't come because she might cry and give us away, and here I am acting like a baby. I hush up. We travel on through swamps, water up to our knees, pulling our feet through muck, crawling through prickle vines. I stub my toe on a rock and fall down. This time I do not scream out."

Chapter 5

Slave Catchers

When a slave escaped, his master would set out to look for him. Most of the time, the master would offer a reward for the return of his slave. These rewards, or **bounties**, encouraged people to become slave catchers. Many slave catchers were poor whites who hunted down runaway slaves for the promise of money.

Once the slaves were caught, they were **flogged** or whipped. John Capehart was a policeman from Norfolk, Virginia, who was hired to flog slaves. When asked in court, "How many negroes do you suppose you have flogged, in all, women and children included?" John Capehart answered, "I don't know how many you have got here in Massachusetts, but I should think I had flogged as many as you've got in the State."

Slave catchers hunted high and low for a runaway slave. They could stop any person of color for questioning. Sometimes, they used bloodhounds to follow the slave's scent. Dogs would chase an escaped slave and bite him, tearing his clothes and skin. Then the slave catcher would take the slave back to his master and collect a reward.

Other times, slave owners would advertise a reward for their missing slaves. On September 22, 1835, a slave owner placed an ad in a local Tennessee newspaper looking for his missing slave. "$250 REWARD. Ran away or stolen . . . on the night of the

16th, Sept., a negro woman named HANNAH. About 40 years old, 5 feet 3 or 4 inches high, thick built, speaks low . . . has a sulky appearance, bushy hair, and wore a blue domestic frock but had other clothes . . . She is most probably in Arkansas making her way up the river."

Advertisement for missing slaves

Anthony Burns was a young slave living in Richmond, Virginia. His master allowed him to earn money by working for others, as long as he gave his master some of his pay. Anthony Burns learned to read and write, but he was not happy because he was still a slave. One day, he used the money he'd earned to board a ship to Boston, Massachusetts. Once he landed in Boston, he was a free man. Or so he thought.

What Anthony didn't realize is that about four years earlier, the Fugitive Slave Act of 1850 was passed. This act required all United States citizens to return escaped slaves to their owners—even slaves who were living in free states.

With the promise of a reward, slave catchers started to look for Anthony Burns. His master eventually found him in Boston, and Anthony was thrown in jail. The people of Boston did not like this; they thought the

Fugitive slaves, Virginia, 1862

Fugitive Slave Act was wrong. An angry mob stormed the courthouse where Anthony was held. Some people offered to buy his freedom. But nothing helped. On June 2, 1854, Anthony Burns was convicted of being a **fugitive** slave and ordered to return to Virginia.

On the day of Burns's departure, a crowd formed outside the courthouse. The crowd grew, and grew, and grew. The United States military and local police were called in to clear the streets. Still, more people came.

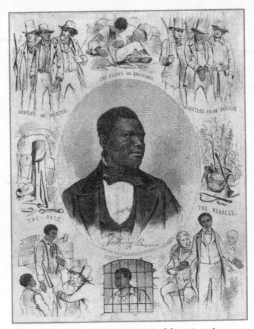

1854 pamphlet about the trial of fugitive slave Anthony Burns

They hung out from windows, peered over balconies, and climbed up on roofs. Fifty thousand people in all came out! More **reinforcements** were called, and a cannon was rolled in. Desperately, the courthouse officials tried to clear a path. Soldiers on horseback swung swords at the crowd. Ignoring the protesters, officials ushered Anthony Burns out of the courthouse and marched him onto a waiting boat. He was returned to slavery.

Lucy Bagby is thought to be the last escaped slave returned to slavery. In 1860, the year before the Civil War started, eighteen-year-old Lucy used the Underground Railroad to escape from West Virginia. She found work as a maid in Cleveland, Ohio, but her former owner found her and had her arrested. A lawyer tried to help Lucy, but the court ordered her to go back to West Virginia. Lucy was once again a slave.

The Fugitive Slave Act also meant that many *free* black men were caught and sold into slavery. Solomon Northup was born in 1808 in Minerva, New York, a free black man. He was a farmer and a great violin player. Solomon was married and had three children. One day, some men offered to pay him to play the violin. But it was a trick. The men kidnapped Solomon and sold him into slavery in

Louisiana. He was beaten and forced to work hard. He tried again and again to get his freedom. He told people he was a free man, but no one listened. One day, an antislavery carpenter named Samuel Bass came to the

SOLOMON IN HIS PLANTATION SUIT.

Solomon Northup

plantation. Samuel believed Solomon's story and helped deliver letters to Samuel's friends in New York to tell them what had happened. Solomon's friends eventually found a lawyer to help Solomon. On January 4, 1853, after spending twelve years as a slave, Solomon was set free.

Northern cities with communities of free black people and former slaves were often destinations for runaway slaves. White abolitionists formed **vigilance committees** in Northern cities, including New York, Boston, Philadelphia, and many others. These committees organized unofficial police forces to keep slave catchers out of their neighborhoods. Although former slaves living in these cities could take some comfort in this form of protection, those traveling on the Underground Railroad had to constantly beware.

A Close Call

"While we running to freedom, me and Momma are on the lookout for slave catchers. But when I see a light ahead, I'm sure it's a lantern for the safe house. I am so excited at the thought of bein' free, that I pull ahead of Momma. I'm running fast— running to freedom! I race toward the light. It ain't the safe house. The light come from a small campfire—with a group of men gathered round it! A gruff voice call out to me, and I turn and see a white man. He wearing a gray jacket and a gray hat. I am face-to-face with a Confederate soldier! He fighting for the South. For slavery. He can send me back to Master Stevens. My heart races. He say to me, 'Boy, fetch me some water.' *Boy?* Then I remember my disguise. He think I am a boy, a boy slave in the Confederate camp. My eyes dart around for the water. I spot the bucket, bring it to him. He drink and lie down, so I lie down, too, at the edge of the camp. When I'm sure he asleep, I creep away to find Momma. She couldn't come into the Confederate camp to rescue me. That would have give us both away! I had to think on my own. Act on my own. We are far from the soldier camp when Momma tell me she's proud of me. She say Poppa would be proud of me, too."

Chapter 6

Conductors

Defying the law, many people secretly helped slaves on their escape routes. These helpers, known as "conductors," hid slaves in their wagons and boats and transported them to the next stop. Some also provided clothing, food, and even medicine. Some conductors were men, others women, some black and some white.

The conductors who worked in the South had particularly dangerous jobs. Sometimes they sneaked into plantations to secretly usher out the slaves and take them north. A lot of conductors were paid by free family members. Others became conductors because they thought it was the right thing to do. All were risking punishment—a conductor who was caught could be fined, jailed, or hanged. Jonathan Walker was a white sea captain who was caught helping slaves escape by boat in Pensacola, Florida. His punishment? A red-hot iron was pressed into his palm and he was branded with the letters "SS," which stood for "slave stealer."

John Fairfield's family owned slaves in Virginia. Growing up, one of his closest friends was a boy named Sam. Sam was a slave owned by the Fairfields. When the boys got older, they took a trip north. Along the way, John pretended Sam was his personal slave. Their act worked, and the pair made it all the way to Canada, where Sam could live as a free man. John Fairfield was probably very happy that he helped his friend make it to freedom, but he knew his job wasn't done. John Fairfield went on to become one of the most daring conductors on the Underground Railroad.

As a conductor, John used acting skills. Sometimes he pretended to be a slave buyer. Other times he claimed he was a slave owner. And at times he posed as a slave catcher. But no matter who he was pretending to be, he always carried a gun. In some cases, he gave the slaves rifles so they would be able to fight if a slave hunter caught up with them. Other times he bought train tickets for the slaves he was helping and they rode north together. Although he helped hundreds of slaves to freedom, sometimes he was caught and sent to jail. But daring John Fairfield broke out of jail several times and continued his work as a conductor.

John Fairfield

Many free blacks and former slaves also worked as conductors on the Underground Railroad. John P. Parker was born into slavery in Norfolk, Virginia. By 1845, he was a free man living in Ripley, Ohio. During the day, he was an ironworker. At night, he was a conductor on the Underground Railroad. Although Ohio was a Northern state, Ripley was mostly pro-slavery, with many slave catchers prowling around, looking for runaways. One day, John Parker heard about a group of slaves hiding in the Kentucky woods. Their leader had been captured, and they were helpless. Volunteering to go on a rescue mission, John Parker put a pair of pistols in his pocket, a knife in his belt, and set out. Deep in the woods, he found the group of ten scared slaves huddled together. Taking command of the group, John Parker led them through the woods, trying to keep them quiet. As they trudged along, branches snapped and popped, echoing through the woods. John Parker feared they would be caught.

One of the men grew desperately thirsty. Although John Parker begged him not to, the thirsty man set off on his own to look for a spring. Suddenly, Parker heard shouts and saw the man being chased by two white men. Parker ordered his group to lie down. Then a shot rang out. John Parker pulled out his gun.

Although the slaves were terrified, no one made a sound. Moments later, John Parker peeked out from the bushes and saw the thirsty man being led by a rope, his arms tied behind his back. The man went to face his punishment alone; he did not betray the rest of the group.

Knowing that they were in more danger than ever, John Parker pressed the group to move faster. They soon arrived at a river where John had arranged for a boat. But when the group arrived, the boat was not yet there. John Parker led them down the banks of the river, hoping to find another boat. At last, they found one, but it only had room for nine. Two men were left on the shore. As the others piled into the boat, a women cried out—her husband was one of the men on the shore, and she did not want to go without him. Selflessly, an unmarried man in the group walked to shore, giving his spot to the woman's husband. As Parker rowed the group to safety, he heard the men on the shore shout. Parker knew this could only mean one thing. The men on shore had been captured, while he and his fugitives were safe.

Harriet Tubman was the most famous conductor on the Underground Railroad. She was born into slavery in Maryland around 1820. When she was little, her master hired her out to another family to watch their baby. Minty (as she was called then) had to sleep on the floor without a mattress or a blanket, and she was whipped if the baby cried. One time, Minty took a sugar cube from the table when no one was looking. She had never tasted sugar before and couldn't help herself. But she knew what she did was wrong, and would surely get whipped. So she ran away and hid in a pigpen. Minty fought with the piglets for scraps. She was cold, and tired, and scared. After five days, Minty couldn't take living with the pigs any longer. Filthy and starving, Minty returned to face her punishment.

By 1849, Minty, who was now known as Harriet, married a free black named John Tubman. Harriet's master died around this time, and she was afraid she would be sold, so she decided to escape to the North. She asked her husband to go with her, but he refused. So Harriet packed some food and a quilt and set out to find freedom. She finally reached Philadelphia, where she found work and tried to save some money. But she was very lonely and she missed her family. So, using the money she saved up, she returned to the South to rescue her family members and other slaves, too. She returned to the South again and again–about nineteen times in all.

Harriet Tubman got the nickname Moses because she was so successful at leading people to freedom, just as Moses is said to have led the **Hebrews** out of slavery in ancient

Harriet Tubman

Egypt. Many people tried to capture her, but they couldn't. If she heard dogs, she kept going. If she saw torches in the woods, she kept going. If she heard shouting behind her, she kept going. She was determined to help other slaves reach freedom.

Not all slaves on the Underground

Railroad had conductors to lead them to freedom. It was a lot harder—and scarier—when runaway slaves were on their own. They could get lost, they could get hurt, they could be captured, they could die. But with or without a conductor, most slaves would take any chance they got to run to freedom.

One resourceful woman escaped from a plantation in Mississippi by herself. One dark night, she bundled together a bit of food and some clothing and stole away to the forest. For several days, she made her way through dense swamps and vine-covered thickets. She knew there were snakes and alligators lurking about, but facing those animals would be better than facing her master's whip.

As the woman traveled, she heard bloodhounds barking and knew that the dogs were tracking her down. Trying to evade them, she found streams to walk in. But still she heard the bloodhounds coming closer. At last she had nowhere to go—she was trapped. She feared the dogs would bite her and leave her bleeding on the forest floor. As the dogs padded closer, the woman reached into her pocket and held out her last crumbs of food. The dogs sniffed her hand, licked up the food, and left.

Safe for now, the woman continued on her journey, which lasted several more months. Along the way, she was helped by conductors of the Underground Railroad until she reached freedom in Canada.

Addy

Journey to Freedom

"Me and Momma got nobody guiding us to freedom. We alone. But we done face the dangers together. Now we standing at a river, and the water fast, rolling. It look angry. Sam, he showed me how to swim, but Momma don't know how. She scared of water. I'm scared, not of the water, but because Momma is. Still, we got no choice—we got to cross that river.

"We hold on to each other tight, but I can feel Momma trembling as we step into the water. Carefully, I try to step 'cross the slippery rocks on the bottom of the river. We 'bout half way 'cross when the water get real fast. It pick up me and Momma and drag us sideways. Momma start to go down, gagging and spitting water from her mouth and nose. A big gush of water hit us. It pull Momma's hand away from mine. Momma is gone! I want to scream, but I take in a huge gulp of air and dive under the dark water. I can't see nothing. I come back up, gulping for air. I call for Momma, but she don't say nothing. I pull in a whole bunch of air and go back under. When I kick out, I feel something soft. It's Momma, trapped in some tree branches under the water. I push and push my feet steady on the branch and wrench Momma free. I pull her to the surface of the water and we both take a gulp of air. Coughing, we make it to the other side of the river. We shaking, wet and cold and tired, but we are together, and we go on."

Chapter 7

Station Houses

Station houses were safe places for run-away slaves to stop and rest along their journey. Some station house owners put a lantern in a window or raised a lantern to the top of a pole as a sign that their house was a safe place. They gave the slaves food and sometimes a change of clothing or a bit of money. There were many different kinds of station houses: barns, attics, cellars, secret rooms in houses, churches, and more.

One of the most famous station houses along the Underground Railroad was the home of Quakers Levi and Catharine Coffin in Newport, Indiana. When Levi Coffin was seven years old, he saw a long line of slaves marching up the road near his house in North Carolina. The slaves were chained together and led by a man holding a whip. Levi's father asked one of the slaves why they were chained. The slave explained that they had been taken away from their wives and children and were chained together so that they couldn't escape and return to their families. Young Levi Coffin was shocked at the way the slaves were being treated. He never forgot what he saw that day.

By 1826, Levi Coffin was married, and he and his wife moved to Newport, Indiana. Coffin worked as a shopkeeper and his business did very well. When he discovered that his two-story, eight-room brick house stood

Levi and Catharine Coffin's house in Indiana

where three routes of the Underground Railroad met—one from Cincinnati, Ohio, one from Madison, Indiana, and one from Jeffersonville, Indiana, he and his wife decided to take action. They opened their home to runaway slaves. Levi Coffin later wrote, "I soon become extensively known to the friends of the slaves, at different points on the Ohio River, where fugitives generally crossed, and to those northward of us on the various routes leading to Canada . . . The roads were always in running order, the connections were good, the conductors active and zealous, and there was (no) lack of passengers. Seldom a week passed without our receiving passengers by the mysterious road . . ."

Anywhere from two thousand to three thousand slaves stopped at the Coffin house on their way north. Slave hunters could track slaves to Newport, but then their trails somehow disappeared. Levi and Catharine's house was often called "Grand Central Station" and Levi Coffin as the "President of the Underground Railroad." They never lost a passenger.

Thomas Garrett was another white abolitionist and Quaker who secretly worked on the Underground Railroad. Born in 1789 in a town called Upper Darby, Pennsylvania, young Thomas witnessed his parents hiding runaway slaves in their home. This was long before the Underground Railroad was established. When Thomas became a grown man, he turned his home in Wilmington, Delaware, into one of the last stations on the Underground Railroad before escaped slaves reached freedom in Pennsylvania. Delaware was a border state that allowed slavery. Thomas Garrett is believed to have given between two thousand and three thousand slaves a safe haven and safe passage.

People who were pro-slavery hated, and feared, Thomas Garrett. Authorities in the neighboring state of Maryland, which also allowed slavery, offered a $10,000 reward for

Thomas Garrett

Thomas Garrett's arrest—a huge sum at that time. Thomas was eventually brought before a **federal court**, where he admitted to helping slaves escape. This time, he did not get off without punishment—he had to pay a heavy fine that took all his money. But he continued to help slaves on their path to freedom. Upon Thomas Garrett's death in 1871, former slaves drew his casket through the streets of Wilmington in an open carriage inscribed with the words "Our Moses."

Many slaves on the run to freedom were afraid to ask strangers for help. They knew that if they knocked on someone's door, they would risk capture. The reward for returning a slave could be more money than a family earned in an entire year. Like everything else on the Underground Railroad, a safe place to stay was found through word of mouth. Slaves sometimes felt safer knocking on the door of a station house owned by a free black or former slave. But no matter which door they knocked on, runaway slaves were always taking a risk that they would be turned in and returned to slavery.

Miss Caroline's Safe House

"Me and Momma are walking along the train tracks when we spot a white house with red shutters up on a little hill. That the house Poppa told us about! Miss Caroline's house. But is it really safe to go there? Me and Momma know we got to take a chance and knock on the door. This old white woman, 'bout the same size as me, open the door a crack. She ain't smiling. She look angry. She tell me to go away. She say, 'Boy, I told you not to come here. Now go back and tell those Confederate soldiers I won't help them.' She think I'm a boy with the Confederate camp, same as the soldier did! I take off my hat and shake out my braids. I tell her that Momma and me running away to freedom, and Uncle Solomon sent us. Miss Caroline's face let go of the anger. She take us inside and give us food, hot baths, and fresh clothes. I get to sleep on a real mattress, not one filled with itchy corn husks. I try to stay awake to think about how good it feels to be clean and safe, but I'm too tired. I just lie in Momma's arms and sleep."

Chapter 8

Abolished!

The Civil War began on April 12, 1861, just one month after Abraham Lincoln took office as the sixteenth president of the United States. Lincoln was firmly against slavery, an issue that ultimately separated the states and helped trigger the war.

Over the next four years, soldiers from the North (the Union army) and the South (the Confederate army) fought each other. The Civil War was one of the bloodiest wars fought in American history. But throughout the war,

President Abraham Lincoln and soldiers on the battlefield near Sharpsburg, Maryland, in October 1862

the Underground Railroad kept running. The conductors kept on guiding runaways, and the station houses continued providing shelter. And gradually, the runaways who made it to freedom started new lives.

On January 1, 1863, President Lincoln issued the **Emancipation Proclamation**, which declared all slaves in Confederate states free. Although this was a first step in ending slavery, slavery wasn't officially abolished until 1865, when the United States Congress approved the Thirteenth Amendment to the Constitution. "Neither slavery nor involuntary servitude . . . shall exist within the United States." With these words, slavery in the United States was abolished, and the Underground Railroad was no longer needed.

It is hard to know exactly how many people traveled on the Underground Railroad. Some say as many as 100,000 slaves sought their freedom this way. With the help of conductors, station masters, and station houses, these slaves found their way out of slave states. The brave passengers and workers on the Underground Railroad were some of the earliest American freedom fighters. They believed that freedom was the right of every human being. Although the Underground

Railroad ended with the Civil War, there are still freedom fighters in the world today carrying on the fight with the belief that all men, women, and children have the right to be free.

The War Is Over

"Boom! Boom! Boom! I wake and sit
straight up in bed. There are loud noises
coming from outside. Poppa (he found his
way back to us!) says it's cannon fire coming from the harbor. Has the war come here
to Philadelphia? But there are also more
noises. People cheering, whistles blowing,
and church bells ringing. My heart beats
faster and faster. I know what's happening!
I jump out of bed and race to the window.
Down below, the street is filled with people.
The war must be over! Momma and Poppa
is crying. I know they crying out of joy. We
get dressed right quick and rush down-
stairs. Someone in the crowd yelling the
North done won the war. All around me,

people laughing, crying, hugging. Some are beating pots and pans and pie tins. Firecrackers pop all round us. It feel like a dream. I lift my face to the sky and see banners waving in the breeze. 'Lincoln and Liberty! One People, One Country,' someone tell me they say. My heart fill up with joy. Our country united again. Now our whole family can be united again. Poppa said he gonna find Esther and Sam and bring them to Philadelphia. We'll be together, and we will be free."

A Note About Addy's Dialect

Connie Porter, the author of the original American Girl Addy historical fiction series as well as the Addy entries in this book, consulted historical studies, slave narratives, and experts to learn how a young enslaved person from South Carolina may have spoken during the antebellum period or before the Civil War.

The language Addy uses is similar to the way many slaves spoke in the 1860s, although it is not exactly the same. You can read real slave narratives from the Civil War era at the Library of Congress website:

Federal Writers' Project: Slave Narrative Project, Vol. 11, North Carolina, Part 1, Adams-Hunter

https://www.loc.gov/item/mesn111

You can also check out these books:

Stolen Childhood: Slave Youth in Nineteenth Century America by Wilma King

Growing Up in Slavery Edited by Yuval Taylor

Glossary

Abolitionist – a person in favor of abolishing, or getting rid of, slavery

Auction – a sale at which things are sold to the person willing to pay the most money

Baying – a low barking or howling

Blacksmith – someone who shapes iron with heat and a hammer

Bounty – money given as a reward

Colony – a settlement in a new country or region

Emancipation Proclamation – President Lincoln's declaration on January 1, 1863, that all slaves in the Confederate states were free

Federal court – the court of the United States government

Flog – to beat with a rod or whip

Founding Fathers – name for the group of men that started the United States of America

Fugitive – someone who runs away

Hebrew – a member of a specific group of ancient people from the areas that are now Israel and Palestine

Middle Passage – the journey slaves were forced to take from Africa across the Atlantic Ocean to the Americas

Mistress – the woman in control of a house

Overseer – a person that directs or manages others

Plantation – a large farm with crops and many workers

Quaker – a member of a specific Christian religious group

Ravine – a small, narrow valley

Reinforcements – extra people sent to strengthen a fighting force

Safe house – a secret place to hide people in danger

Till – to plow

Vigilance committee – a group of people that form an unofficial police force

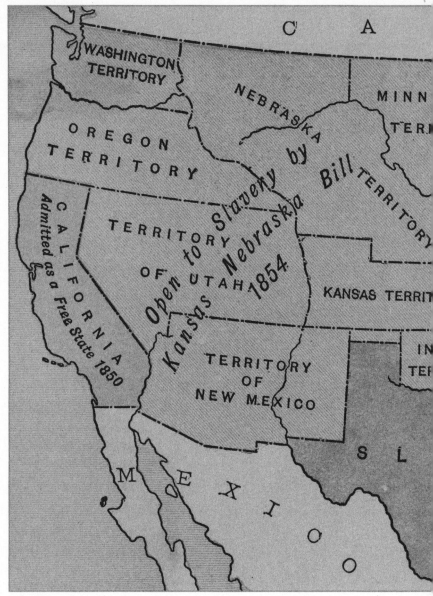

United States prior to the Civil War; slave states vs. free states in 1854

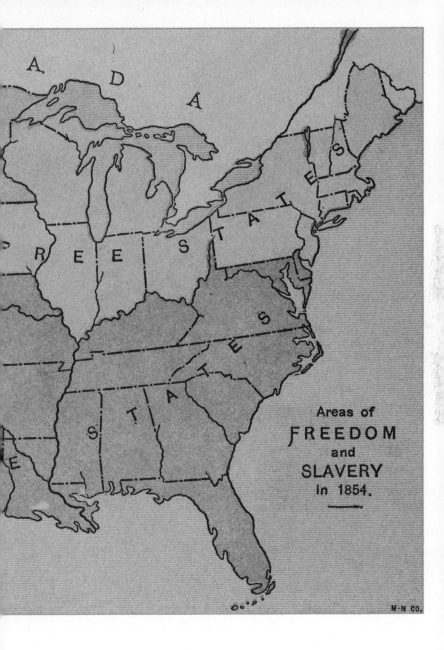

Areas of
FREEDOM
and
SLAVERY
In 1854.

M-N CO.

Timeline

1619 – Twenty Africans are brought to Jamestown, Virginia, and sold as slaves

1797 – Sojourner Truth is born into slavery and given the name Isabella Baumfree

1804 – By this year, slavery is outlawed in Connecticut, Massachusetts, New Hampshire, New Jersey, New York, Pennsylvania, Rhode Island, and Vermont

1808 – It becomes illegal to bring slaves into the United States from different countries

1830 – Josiah Henson follows the North Star from Maryland to Canada

1831 – Tice Davids escapes from Kentucky to Ohio; William Lloyd Garrison publishes a newspaper called *The Liberator*

1833 – William Lloyd Garrison co-founds the Anti-Slavery Society

1841 – Frederick Douglass speaks at an Anti-Slavery Society meeting in Nantucket, Massachusetts

1842 – Sixteen-year-old Caroline Quarlls makes a daring escape north from Missouri

1845 – Frederick Douglass publishes his autobiography, *Narrative of the Life of Frederick Douglass: An American Slave*

1849 – Harriet Tubman escapes to freedom; Henry Brown travels to Philadelphia inside a box to be free

1850 – Fugitive Slave Act is passed

1853 – Solomon Northup is declared free after spending twelve years as a slave

1854 – Anthony Burns is returned to slavery in West Virginia

1860 – Lucy Bagby is thought to be the last escaped slave returned to slavery

1861 – The Civil War begins

1863 – President Lincoln delivers the Emancipation Proclamation

1865 – The Civil War ends; the Thirteenth Amendment to the U.S. Constitution is passed, ending slavery

Source Notes

Adler, David A. *Harriet Tubman and the Underground Railroad.* New York, New York: Holiday House, 2013.

Africans in America: Judgment Day. Boston, Massachusetts. WGBH Educational Foundation/PBS Online, 1998.

Bial, Raymond. *The Underground Railroad.* Boston, Massachusetts: Houghton Mifflin Company, 1995.

Carson, Mary Kay. *Which Way to Freedom? And Other Questions About . . . The Underground Railroad.* New York, New York: Sterling Children's Books, 2014.

Fradin, Dennis Brindell. *The Underground Railroad.* New York, New York: Marshall Cavendish Benchmark, 2009.

Isaacs, Sally Senzell. *Life on the Underground Railroad.* Chicago, Illinois: Heinemann Library, 2002.

McDonough, Yona Zeldis. *What Was the Underground Railroad?* New York, New York: Grosset & Dunlap, 2013.

Porter, Connie. *American Girl Beforever: A Heart Full of Hope, A classic featuring Addy, Volume 2.* Middleton, Wisconsin: American Girl Publishing, 2014.

Porter, Connie. *American Girl Beforever: Finding Freedom, A classic featuring Addy, Volume 1.* Middleton, Wisconsin: American Girl Publishing, 2014.

Raatma, Lucia. *The Underground Railroad.* New York, New York: Scholastic Inc., 2012.

Stein, R. Conrad. *Escaping Slavery on the Underground Railroad.* Berkeley Heights, New Jersey: Enslow Publishers, Inc., 2008.

Stein, R. Conrad. *The Underground Railroad.* New York, New York: Children's Press, 1997.

Stowe, Harriet Beecher. *A Key to Uncle Tom's Cabin: Presenting the Original Facts and Documents Upon Which the Story Is Founded.* New York, New York: Dover Publications, 2015.